KARATE

TICKY DONOVAN

PELHAM BOOKS · LONDON

First published in Great Britain by
Pelham Books Ltd
27 Wrights Lane
London W8 5TZ
1984
Reprinted 1987

© Ticky Donovan 1984

ISBN 0 7207 1535 0

Printed and bound in Great Britain by
Butler & Tanner Limited, Frome, Somerset

Acknowledgements

The author gratefully acknowledges the help and assistance given by David Mitchell in the production of the text.
Special thanks also go to British internationals Alfie Borg
and Mick Layzelle for their patience and assistance in the
production of the pictures.

Contents

Foreword by David Mitchell

In the twenty or so years that I have practised karate I have come across a few people who appeared to be able to score on me at will yet were able to negate my own attempts. Seemingly I was just one big target for them to practise whatever technique happened to come into their heads, whilst they remained just outside the range of my efforts. It was all the more infuriating because everything I did seemed to be anticipated and my attempts to even up the score seemed to lead me deeper and deeper into trouble!

Many is the time I have sat on the sidelines and watched Ticky Donovan doing a graceful (and painless!) demolition job on some aspiring British squad member. Feeling enthused by the display, I've gone to my own club and practised with the high grades there – but with a significant lack of progress. I now know that karate competition is like a game of chess. It's not just a case of throwing a technique at a target and hoping for the best. The successful fighter uses one technique to set up another, in exactly the same way that the snooker player pots his target but then leaves the white exactly positioned for the next shot. Natural fighters can achieve some of this instinctively; they don't have to think it all out laboriously in their heads. Here is an example of someone – a natural fighter – who has analysed precisely what he is doing right and set it down in the form of a manual.

This book by Ticky Donovan is the first-ever book about how to win karate matches. He goes far beyond a simple compendium of useful tricks and explains how even the most elementary techniques can have their scoring potential enhanced by a few simple adjustments. The person who reads this book and takes up its suggestions will find his or her fighting improved; of that, there is no doubt. It doesn't matter whether the reader is a British international or a green belt in a provincial club, this book will provide some clues and hints that will result in a better performance.

Ticky does not, however, offer any easy way. The road to improvement is a hard one. The reader must accept that the proper application of these principles takes a great deal of practice. It's no use having to consciously think about correct line or distance; the concept must be practised until it becomes automatic. Only when that stage is reached will the true benefits of this book become apparent. It is curious to see the western mind grappling with the concept of Zen – the state of no preconceptions that is vital to the performance of karate. The Japanese originators never managed to get this concept across and it has been left to an East Londoner to explain this basic principle in a way we can all understand.

Ticky Donovan is an ex-international and member of the British team that won the world championships in 1975 at Long Beach, California. He has won many national tournaments and set up his own karate organisation called the British Ishin Ryu Karate Association. 'Ishin Ryu' means 'Of One Mind' and Ticky holds the rank of 6th Dan, awarded by the English Karate Federation.

Soon after it was founded, members of the Ishin Ryu began appearing in the line-up for prizes at prestigious tournaments. Not only did they do well in fighting, they also won kata events, showing the breadth of excellence produced by Ticky Donovan. He has been called the best coach in the world by the chairman of the World Union of Karate Organisations (WUKO), Jacques Delcourt. He has received trophies, certificates and commendations from all over the world and is the undisputed master of competition karate.

As an aside, his effect upon the rules of competition has been major. As a ruthless coach it is necessary to know the rules of competition, but more important than that the coach must have a deep understanding of the principles underlying the rules. His rigorous challenging of questionable decisions has made referees and judges more aware of their standards. As one of Britain's two representatives to the first-ever WUKO Technical Congress, he was instrumental in effecting major and far-reaching changes in the rules, to the benefit of subsequent generations of sport karate fighters.

There may be great coaches after Ticky Donovan, but let there be no doubt that he was the first. Those who come after may well build upon his theories, but it was Ticky Donovan who first recognised and set out the basic principles of successful competition karate.

August 1984

David Mitchell
Member of:
English Karate Federation
English Karate Council
British Karate Federation
Martial Arts Commission
European Karate Union
    Directing Committee
World Union of Karate
    Organisations Directing
    Committee

Introduction

The most important thing that a fighter needs to succeed is ambition. Without the will to win there will not be the motivation needed to begin a rigorous training programme. The fighter must be prepared to train regularly and hard – twice or three times a week is not enough. It doesn't matter if the club is only twice a week because in training to win at competition karate, there is a need to build up stamina and this can only be done by regular roadwork, or any other form of good aerobic exercise. The competition fighter sometimes has to call up great reserves of strength and stamina in order to keep up the pressure. For this reason, he must be fit and have a good capacity for work.

Practising techniques until they become perfect is the goal and it will be difficult to achieve this if the fighter runs out of wind. The unfit fighter's training schedule will be less rigorous and therefore improvement will be slower. Fighters need to look after their physical condition and it is very important that they avoid alcohol, cigarettes and the wrong type of food.

The successful competitor needs very few training aids. A large mirror is one of the most important and a good bag is useful, if there is somewhere to hang it. When using the mirror the fighter must have room to move around; he must move very quickly, almost as though he was trying to beat his reflection to the move.

Most people have a 'good' and a 'bad' side, but the successful competitor can't afford to. The bad side must receive extra training until it is better than the so-called good side. In some cases, people who have practised hard on their weak sides end up with that side better than the favoured one!

Many fighters have favourite techniques. This too is a bad thing

Ticky Donovan with some of the trophies he's won

and must be avoided. Successful fighters come under close scrutiny and any reliance they place on favoured techniques will be seen and used against them. It is much better to achieve a good, all-round competence. By this means, the fighter can match a larger spectrum of opponents without having to rely upon a small number of techniques that may be inappropriate. Not only techniques, but tactics too must be flexible. Defensive opponents, aggressive opponents and southpaws all need different tactics. A fighter who is good only at attacking is half as good as he could be if he worked harder on his defence tactics!

Many fighters spend a long time on free fighting. This is not a good thing because the techniques that work in free fighting don't always work in competition karate. In free fighting there is nothing to lose, since no points are being awarded. This factor can encourage the fighter to become sloppy and less single-minded. The sheer informality of free sparring makes it very different indeed from competing to win!

Some fighters are good losers. Good losers are advised to save their money and not buy this book! This book is all about winning and winning well. Some people have lost before they begin to fight. This often happens where a newcomer to competition meets up with last year's champion. A point to consider is that the latter has everything to lose and the newcomer has nothing; so there is no reason why such people shouldn't go all out to win. Good losers give up easily when they are a point down in a match. This is a nonsense. There are many cases where someone has come from way behind to become the eventual winner simply because they maintained pressure right up to the time-up bell.

Once upon a time, when there was only one point to be won, people who got a half-point lead sat back and let the opponent come to them. With the new six half-points rules this attitude cannot be continued and fighters must now go and score, score, score, right up to the bell. The name of the game is aggression – from start to finish. In this book I have put down for the first time my recipe for success in competition karate. I feel confident that by studying it and practising hard the reader will gain a new insight into the techniques of winning.

David 'Ticky' Donovan
East Ham, London

August 1984

An Introduction to the Rules of Karate Competition

Karate competition began in Japan during the late 1940s. Originally, karate was thought to be too dangerous to form the basis of a sport and so all practice was done through prearranged sparring and katas. Prearranged sparring is where two partners take it in turns to attack and defend; they use a set attack and a set defence, so there is little possibility of injury. Katas are sequences of karate techniques performed against the empty air; the kata exponent visualizes imaginary attackers and deals with them through multiple prearranged sequences.

However, these two avenues did not satisfy the karate exponents who began to perform faster and faster prearranged sparring routines and eventually started to make the attacks realistic and spontaneous. From there it was only a small step to competition. The early karateka must have looked at Kodokan judo and seen how the unarmed martial art of ju-jitsu had been forged into a sport form. They turned their attention upon karate and by stripping away the obviously hazardous techniques, like spearhand to the eyes and kicking to the knee, and by landing others with limited force on scheduled target areas of the opponent's body, they achieved the first form of competition karate.

Since then, there has been a rapid evolution towards more open fighting. The old single-point scoring system has been replaced with a three-point, or six half-point bout and this has encouraged fighters to go for more advanced techniques.

Karate matches are normally fought on matted areas which measure eight metres along each side. Inside these areas are four lines upon which stand the two fighters and the two refereeing officials. One fighter wears a red belt and the other a white belt. An arbitrator sits just to the side of the area. His function is to check

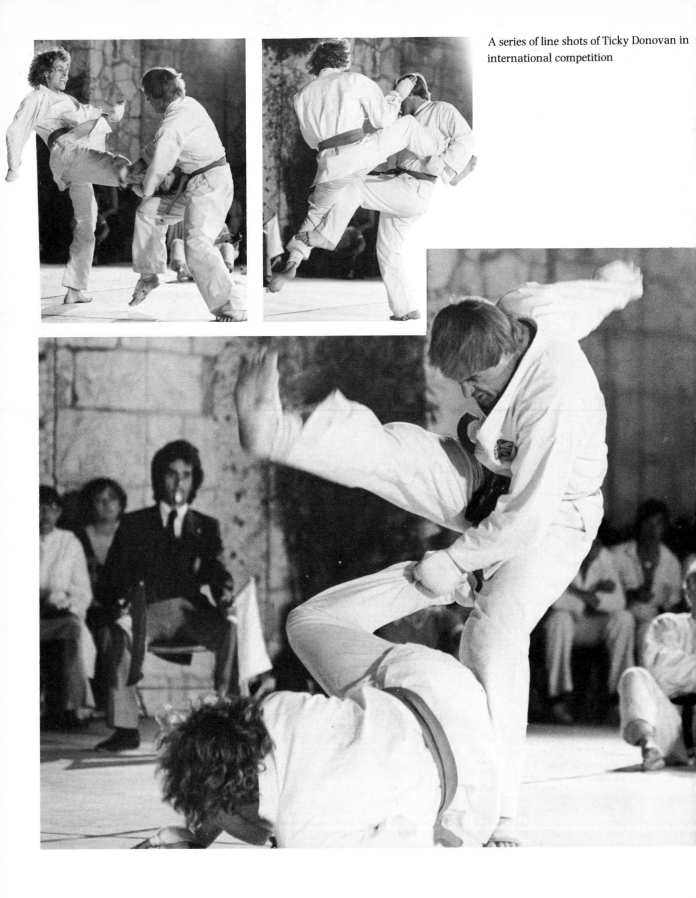

A series of line shots of Ticky Donovan in international competition

17

that all the rules are properly applied. In the past he was asked to check judgments on score or penalty, but this is a bad practice and should be avoided.

The referee runs the match and awards all scores and penalties. He is assisted by a judge. During the match both officials move freely around the area and try to keep exactly opposite each other, so that each has a different field of view. Scores and penalties are awarded by agreement between these two and this agreement usually takes the form of gestures. It is important to avoid conversation between the officials since this can lead to lengthy interruptions in the match.

Matches are two or three minutes of actual fighting time and the clock is stopped whenever there is an interruption. When there are 30 seconds to go the timekeeper gives a short audible signal, and at time-up the signal is of longer duration. The object is for a fighter to score three full points, six half points, or a combination of the two totalling three full points. To score a full point a fighter must deliver a perfect technique to a scoring area of the opponent's body. Perfect form is difficult to achieve and near-perfect scores receive a half-point award.

In some cases a near-perfect technique can be given a full point. For this to happen, the score must have been made to the opponent's undefended back, or a difficult combination of techniques used. Kicks to the head tend to score full points because they are technically more difficult than a punch to the chest.

Competition karate is often referred to as 'non-contact'. This is a misnomer: scoring techniques may land with fairly considerable force, having regard to the area attacked. Whilst full force is frowned upon, some fighters get the occasional good thump in the stomach that can literally drop them to the floor – and a score will still be given if the circumstances are right! Contact to the face and head, though, requires much greater control and only a touch contact is allowed.

Kicking to the groin or attacking the eyes are not allowed. There is a schedule of prohibited actions and any fighter found infringeing a rule can be either warned, receive a half-point penalty, a full-point penalty or be disqualified. In severe cases the fighter can be disbarred from the tournament. The normal practice is to first give a warning for a slight infringement, then if the fighter repeats that particular infringement he or she is penalised by giving a half point to the opponent. By this means, the penalties awarded gradually increase in severity. If an infringement is particularly blatant, the referee can miss out the warning and the half-point penalty and go direct to a full-point penalty or even a disqualification. It is worth noting that the coach's behaviour is also important. Bad behaviour from the coach can result in his fighter receiving a penalty.

At the end of each match the referee gives a verdict. A half-point lead is sufficient to indicate victory but where the scores are identical other factors may be considered. The referee will consider whether one fighter used better techniques, or was more spirited. If he thinks so, then the match can be given to that fighter. Unfortunately, few referees use this alternative and wrongly give a draw, or ask the fighters to compete in an extension where the first to score is the winner. In team matches there is an odd number of fighters in each team and the one with the highest number of individual match successes is the winner. Where the teams tie on match wins, then the points score is totalled and the team with the greater number of points wins. When this too is tied, extra matches and extensions are fought until the tie is finally broken.

During the course of a match one of the contestants may become injured. When this happens the doctor is called to give first aid. Bad referees ask the doctor to guess at the force used in causing the injury. This is quite wrong. The referee should be paying attention and know how hard a blow actually was, without having to ask someone else. If a fighter receives a blow to the head that knocks him or her down, then that fighter must be medically withdrawn and cannot take part in any further fighting for a specified number of weeks.

Other rules affect the validity of techniques when they are performed outside of the match area. If any contestant leaves the area during the running of a match he or she will be warned. If they do it again a penalty is awarded as previously described. An exception to the rule is when someone is literally pushed out of the area by the opponent. The situation gets more complicated if a fighter scores and then leaves the area. Provided that there is a score, then the exit is not counted because the referee will have called a halt at the instant of the score and the exit thus occurred after an order to stop the match was made. On the other hand, if a fighter uses a technique which does not score and during the execution of that technique he inadvertently steps outside the area, then that exit will count because the referee, not seeing a score, won't have called for a halt.

This stopping of the match every time that a score or penalty is to be awarded can be infuriating. The Chief Referee of WUKO, George Anderson, defines a referee's job as that of stopping the match every time it becomes interesting! This is a regrettable fact, but without it karate competition would become simply a mêlée of techniques, with one running into the other and no clear scores. Obviously there is a need to halt the match from time to time and the good refereeing panel will ensure that those halts are no more frequent than is necessary. When a halt is called, the action must be restarted as soon as possible.

There are interesting developments taking place in karate competition but these will in no way reduce the effectiveness of the techniques and principles described in this book.

General Principles

To be successful on the competition area, the fighter needs to analyse exactly what goes into successful competition, starting with the very basic techniques – the building blocks, or alphabet, of basic moves – then going on to the combination techniques which link the basic technique alphabet into words. The idea of a combination technique is to face the opponent with a bewildering series of moves, each of which has to be countered separately. One technique must follow another in rapid and logical succession.

No matter what the situation, the good competition fighter will find himself always on the right foot and with a technique ready and waiting. To achieve this goal the fighter must build up conditioned reflexes that do not require thinking about. When driving a car a whole series of complex moves is carried out without any kind of conscious thought. This is because, by repetition, those moves have been built in to the body. Constant practice is the way karate reflexes are acquired.

A mirror is one of the best training aids to use. It shows openings that the fighter may not be aware of. By using a mirror the fighter sees himself through his opponent's eyes and can take the necessary steps to correct deficiencies in guard, posture, or technique. Another valuable training aid is the bag. A lot of karate practice takes place against the empty air and techniques can become unreal. Using a bag shows up failings in technique and also improves timing and distance. The actual sensation of hitting a target is useful in that it makes sure that fists are correctly formed and toes pulled back out of harm's way.

Practising with a colleague is a good idea as long as he is trustworthy and there are no spectators about. It is also a good thing not to start one's competition career off too early. Before going into

Ticky Donovan (left) with Dominique Valera. The author specially acknowledges the inspiration and help given by Dominique Valera

the area, the competitor should have mastered the basic techniques themselves. The 'alphabet' must be learned before the fighter can compete without serious risk of injury.

Competition karate is like a game of snooker. The object is not only to pot a ball but to leave the table cued up for the next shot. For maximum versatility, the fighter must learn many techniques and this is where the coach comes in. There are many coaches who happen to have good kicks and they try to force their students to become good kickers too, even when they are clearly not cut out to be. On the other hand, the good coach will operate a two-way learning process: he learns from the student, as well as coaching him. By this means, the coach finds out his students' strengths and weaknesses and is able to structure their coaching to bring about an improvement.

Tactics

It is useful to know what kind of fighter one's opponent is so that techniques can be used which are applicable. Therefore, from the very start of the match the tactical fighter will test his opponent. He will use abrupt stance changes and move rapidly around the area. A sudden stamp on the front foot may fool the opponent into thinking an attack is imminent. If the opponent digs in or makes to come forward, then he is an attacking fighter. If he backs off, then he is a defensive or nervous fighter.

With fighters who dig in their heels, the tactic to use is aggression. Attacking fighters are not always too good on defence and so they should be kept under constant pressure. Thus, the clever fighter will provide an opening for attack only to close it off and counter-attack at the last minute.

Nervous fighters should be pursued hard, with reliance placed on feints and flurries of movement that cause confusion. The double shuffle, or run-in reverse punch, is ideal for use against such fighters. The shuffle is best performed by shorter people – taller ones tend to get tangled up in their own legs.

Distance and line must always be in the favour of the tactical fighter. Opponents who favour kicks will tend to fight from further away than those who prefer punches. It is important to be able to adapt to the opponent, rather than strictly fighting according to one rigid system only.

Sometimes it is a good idea to give the opponent an opening to attack. A nervous and closed fighter is very difficult to deal with and he should be drawn out into committing himself by means of target lures.

A great many fighters wait overly long to deliver a technique, even when they are in range for it. When there is a good chance of a surprise move succeeding it should be used. For example, when two people are in reverse punch range of each other, the first to punch will have the element of surprise on his side and may well score. If there is only an even chance, or less, of a technique succeeding, then it shouldn't be used.

The fighter must be prepared to work hard from the start of the match to the very end. It is tempting to ease the pressure off when ahead but this is a bad mistake in today's competition. Every opportunity must be exploited so that the next person in line to fight is daunted by reports he has heard.

The match must be opened in a fluid and open way, with the fighter adjusting to his opponent as previously described. However, when a good points lead has been built up, the fighter can return to favourite or spectacular techniques.

The fighter must always make sure that he uses techniques that actually work and not ones he wishes did! As a side issue, the coach's behaviour must also be considered in a tactical sense. Because he is situated a little further back from the match he often sees what his fighter misses. It is a bad habit, however, for the coach to call the technique to be used in plain English. Many is the time that the coach has called 'front kick' to his fighter but unfortunately, the opponent has also heard the advice and is ready and waiting for it. A code must be developed which is known only to that particular coach and his fighters.

The most worrying time for any coach is during the match extension – or 'sudden death'. In this the first to score wins the match. There is no room for a mistake during the extension and the outcome is always uncertain. At best, a fighter only has a fifty per cent chance of winning in a sudden-death situation.

The fighter who prefers to attack must practise defence and vice versa; in this way, it is possible to double one's capabilities. Training must be rigorously followed and the sensible fighter will work up a training programme for a particular tournament. This programme will ensure that he is physically and mentally ready on the night. After the event, a good rest is in order. Too much training can take the edge off a performance and lead to a fighter becoming stale.

Remember these three important points:

1 The opponent will respond to what he sees – or what he thinks he sees.

2 The object is to score on the opponent.

3 The opponent must not be allowed to score.

Stance

FIG. 1A

FIGS. 1A AND B – CORRECT STANCE

The stance is the platform from which techniques are delivered. It has to be fluid, never still for an instant. Freezing the movement would show a middle to longish stance with the weight spread fifty/fifty on both feet. This particular weight distribution allows rapid movement in all directions. It is an unspecialized stance that can be used either to launch an attack or to dig in as the attacker rushes in. A longer stance leads to slowness of movement and a higher stance is open to techniques slipping in under the guard. The fifty/fifty stance favours both kickers and punchers and its very length removes the possibility of a double legsweep.

Many fighters bounce up and down as they square up. This is a bad thing and they can be run out of the area if attacked hard. The stance must be fairly strong and have about two fist-widths of sidestep when the rear knee is dropped down to the floor and measured against the front heel. Less sidestep makes the fighter susceptible to a footsweep and more leaves the groin open.

The fighter must never stand square-on and facing the opponent. This presents a broad band of target area for him to aim at and at the same time removes penetration from the reverse punch. With this in mind, the fighter should turn forty-five degrees on to the opponent. This angle is fairly critical: when turned too far away the reverse punch hand is pulled so far back as to be unusable; when the correct angle is achieved there is only a thin slice of body open as a target and the reverse-punch hand is left cocked and waiting.

The arms must be kept in motion, since they are used both to obscure the opponent's view and to distract him. The rear hand is held back at waist level. It is kept open and loose so it can be quickly

FIG. 1B

used as a block or reverse punch. In principle, the front arm is held well out from the body and kept open. In this position it can stop potential attacks close to their source and before they develop their full power. Some schools of traditional karate teach students to keep their front arms close to the body. However, in competition this is not a good thing because it leaves only a short distance in which to deflect the by now fast-moving technique. The position of the front arm is very important where the attacker has taken the initiative and only the defender's reflexes can save him from being scored on.

Line

FIG. 3A

FIGS. 2A AND B – INCORRECT

Expressed simply, line is the relationship of one fighter's stance to another's. With the correct use of line, it is possible for one fighter to increase his chance of scoring, whilst diminishing his opponent's. In practice, what this means is standing with the front foot slightly outside the opponent's front foot. If the opponent tries to reverse punch now he has to turn his hips more than is safe. Even with the hips turned fully, it is still possible for the punch to glance off without scoring. Yet a further drawback in this example of bad line is that the punch itself has to travel a greater distance and can be more easily blocked.

FIGS. 3A AND B – CORRECT

Though the opponent's line may be bad and his technique impaired, the same is definitely not the case for the fighter with good line. In his case, the reverse punch is almost certain to score because there is a wider target – the punch doesn't have to travel so far and it is harder to block.

FIGS. 4A, B AND C – BAD LINE

This is even more clearly shown in the case of a kick attack. The

FIG. 2A

FIG. 2B

FIG. 3B

FIG. 4A

FIG. 4B

FIG. 4C

FIG. 5A

FIG. 5B

FIG. 5C

FIG. 6A

FIG. 6B

FIG. 6C

FIG. 6D

fighter on the left tries to use a roundhouse kick but his line is bad at the outset. As soon as his foot lifts off, he turns square on to the opponent, presenting a large target to be attacked. The opponent sees the target and hits it with a reverse punch to gain a possible full point.

FIGS. 5A, B AND C — GOOD LINE

There's no reason why a roundhouse kick should not be used to open an attack, but the first thing to check is that the line is good. The fighter on the right has good line. His foot is not inside the opponent's. Because of this, as his foot lifts off, there is no target for the opponent to go for. Note the correct use of the kick, with the body leaning away from the possibility of a counterattack. The knee is brought across high and a forward guard is maintained.

FIGS. 6A, B, C AND D

The fighter on the left has bad line and is attempting a front kick. Because of his bad line, when the kick is blocked it falls inside the opponent's front leg. From this position, all it takes is for the landing front foot to be hooked away and a score is there for the taking.

When using a kick, remember to always deliver it from a good line so that, if blocked, it falls to the outside of the opponent's foot where it can be used to hook him. There is, however, one exception to this maxim and that can be found on page 109.

Creating an Opening

Creating an opening and then using it is an easy way to pick up a point or two.

FIGS. 7A AND B
A snap punch is aimed at the opponent's face causing him to blink reflexively. The punch is deliberately aimed to the side of his face and this causes him to bring his front hand across thus blocking his own view. This technique is often used as an opener for a follow-up reverse punch or second snap punch, using the defender's own blocking arm to obscure his view of the counter.

FIGS. 8A, B, C AND D
The fighter on the left uses a back fist off the rear hand to the side of his opponent's face. Because the strike goes to the side of the head, the defender's block obscures his vision to the quickly following front kick that strikes high under the arm and to the side of the body.

FIG. 8A

FIG. 8B

FIG. 7A

FIG. 7B

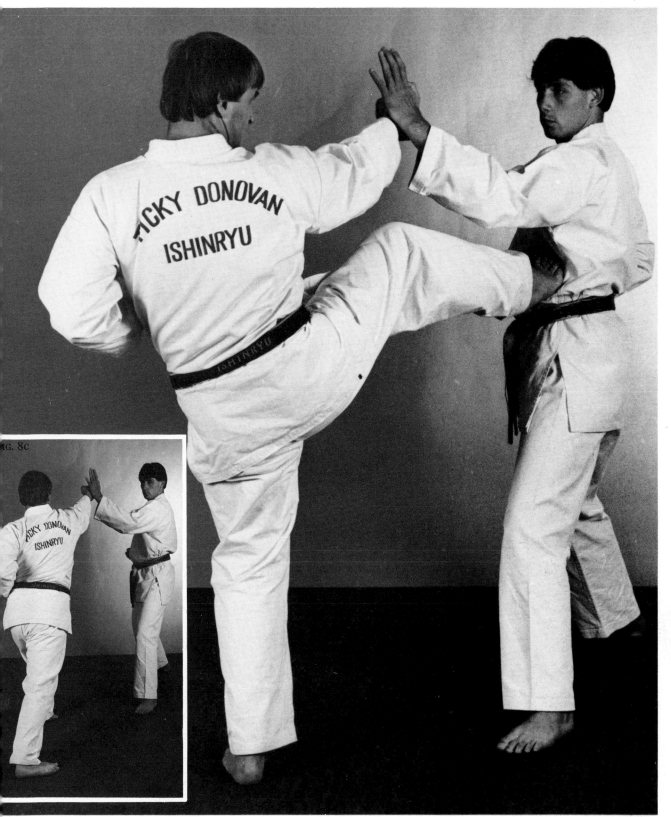

FIG. 8c

FIG. 8d

Snap Punch

FIGS. 9A, B AND C

The snap punch comes off the front fist and is similar to the jab used in boxing. To deliver it, the body swivels forty-five degrees on to the opponent and weight is put on the front foot. With good line, the angle of the body narrows the opponent's chance for a counter yet leaves reverse punch available for use as a follow-up. The rear hand must be kept high so as to protect the jaw.

As was mentioned in the previous section, a straight punch into the face causes a reflex flinch and use can be made of this in a quick follow-up strike. A useful combination incorporating a snap punch is to aim to one side of the face, then, as the opponent's guard swings across, take a short step and snap punch off the other hand from a slightly different angle.

FIG. 9A

By using hip twist as the snap punch is put in, the rear foot can slide further out of line, allowing a safe follow-up using a reverse punch. At the same time, both the opponent's snap punch is made to miss and his reverse punch taken too far out of play.

Although effective techniques, snap punches are not often scored in competition karate.

FIG. 9B

FIG. 10A

FIG. 10B

FIG. 10C

FIG. 10D

Reverse Punch

FIGS. 10A, B, C AND D

Reverse punch is the single most effective technique in competition karate. It can be used on its own or in combination with other moves, to attack the head, face or body. Because of the forward shift in weight, strong hip twist and distance over which the punch accelerates, reverse punch is very strong. During the delivery the front foot can slide forwards, thus deepening the stance and extending its range. The hips must turn square on and no more, otherwise the punch will be weak and over-extended.

The shoulders rotate with the hips and in so doing reduce the area open to the opponent's counter. The heel of the rear foot can lift off the ground – there is no need to stick with traditional dogma that states that the back leg must be rigid: it's far more important to get weight in behind the punch.

FIGS. 11A, B, C AND D

When within punching range, there's no point in hanging back. The first to punch will generally score and this is especially the case when fighting a southpaw. In this latter situation the first to punch closes off the other's reverse punch and only one can score. The person who attacks first has the advantage, and if his line is good then the possibility of a score is very strong.

FIGS. 12A, B AND C

The reverse punch can be used in many different ways and is a truly versatile technique. Here its use is seen against someone who stands their ground when challenged. The fighter on the left quickly steps forward whilst holding his front fist motionless. If the opponent doesn't retreat, the forward fist can be turned into a fast reverse punch. Note that during the step forward the attacker's foot comes to lie outside of the opponent's – the reason for this will be seen later on. When doing this technique, it is also important to

FIG. 12A

FIG. 12B

FIG. 12C

make sure that the front hand doesn't move at all during the step. It must be held well forward at all times. Also note that the attacker does not lead with his chin when stepping forwards.

FIGS. 13A, B AND C

In this sequence the start is exactly the same but this time the opponent is a nervous type who steps quickly back. In this case the first reverse punch is used as before but it is followed with a further step and a follow-up reverse punch to a lower target. Note again

FIG. 13A

FIG. 13B

FIG. 13C

FIG. 14A

FIG. 14B

FIG. 14C

FIG. 14D

that the attacker's foot finishes to the outside of the opponent's. Both reverse punches are delivered at different heights and this causes a degree of confusion to the opponent. Wherever possible, it is always better to vary the height of successive attacks in order to reduce the chance of them being blocked.

FIGS. 14A, B, C AND D
When attacking a strong defensive fighter it is a good idea to draw him out by giving him an opening. That's exactly what the fighter on the left is doing. The front hand is held still as he runs in with the first step. His first punch is blocked by the opponent who refuses to back off a step. Seemingly to tempt providence, the attacker pushes his hips forward and presents a broad target for counter-attack. However, when the opponent looses a reverse punch, the attacker sways back out of range with his hips, simultaneously knocking down the punch and counterpunching to his face.

FIGS. 15A, B AND C
In a similar way, the reverse punch can be used to score when following a snap punch. The fighter on the left slides forward and snap punches to the opponent's face. The slide forward takes him

FIG. 15A

FIG. 15B

FIG. 15C

close to the opponent's front foot and the snap punch goes to the side of the face, bringing the block across. The target is then quickly changed and the snap punch pulled back to be replaced with a reverse punch to the mid-section. The change from snap punch to reverse punch must be very quick, using as it does the reflex blink of the opponent's eyes caused by the snap punch and his own obscuring block.

FIGS. 16A, B AND C

In this sequence timing is of the essence. The opponent is a good counterattacker and so the fighter on the right does not step forwards with the snap punch. As expected, the opponent immediately counters, but because there has been no slide forwards his reverse punch falls short. As it is being pulled back, the attacker drops his hips and moves forwards on his front leg, aiming a mid-section reverse punch into the side of the body. This last punch actually follows the opponent's failed counter as it is withdrawn.

High/low sequences are very good in competition and whereas snap punches tend not to be scored so often, the reverse punch following almost certainly will be. When a strong reverse punch

FIG. 16A

FIG. 16B

FIG. 16C

follows an effective snap punch, there is a possibility of scoring a full point because an effective combination technique has been used. The reverse sequence is not so successful because, first of all, there is no initial reflex flinch produced by the snap punch and, secondly, the technique should finish decisively and a solid reverse punch to the body is more definitive than a controlled snap punch.

FIGS. 17A, B, C AND D

The **double shuffle** is the name given to a technique that is used to cover ground quickly. The flurry of movement confuses the opponent and allows a reverse punch to score. The fighter on the left snap punches to the opponent's face. In the same instant he brings his front leg back and the rear leg forwards in a hop. This hop does not cover ground and as it completes, the attacker runs forwards and drives in a mid-section reverse punch. Again there is a high/low sequence, where the opponent's first block obscures his own vision momentarily. The simultaneous hop and punch completely mislead the opponent.

FIGS. 18A, B AND C

Here is another example of providing a target to draw out the

FIG. 17A

FIG. 17B

FIG. 17C

FIG. 17D

FIG. 18A

FIG. 18B

FIG. 18C

FIG. 19A

FIG. 19B

FIG. 19C

FIG. 20A

FIG. 20B

FIG. 20C

FIG. 20D

opponent. The fighter on the right lifts his front guard and thrusts his hips forward. Immediately, the opponent throws a reverse punch but it is countered with a simultaneous knock-down block and reverse punch counter. Note that the fighter on the right draws back his body from danger as he counters.

FIGS. 19A, B AND C

Line is important when dealing with a reverse punch attack. The fighter on the left has his front foot in line with the opponent's rear foot. As the reverse punch comes in, the fighter on the left jumps quickly to the left and twists his hips. Note that the punch is deflected by the forearm and the way the blocking arm is bent sets it up ready to use as a snap punch, or a back fist to the face. When two fighters have this line, the attacking punch tends to come into the centre of the body.

FIGS. 20A, B, C AND D

Note here that the fighter on the left has a slightly different line. His front foot lies approximately between his opponent's sidestep. With this line, the attacking punch will come into the side of the body. To counter it the fighter on the left uses a rapid movement of his rear leg to pull his body diagonal to the attack. Combined with this sudden move is a strong and simultaneous block and counter-punch. It is important that the block and counter occur simultaneously.

In both cases, the direction of movement taken during evasion prevents the opponent from using an easy follow-up.

FIG. 21A

FIG. 21B

48

Back Fist

Back fist is a useful technique. It uses a combination of hip action and a loose elbow and wrist joint, both of which tighten on impact to give a 'snap'. Back fist can be used either off the front hand or off the rear hand. An example of its use from the rear hand is seen on page 34 where its use to the side of the opponent's head causes 'overblocking' and an opening for front kick is provided.

To deliver a back fist, the striking elbow should be lifted high and the hips should rotate away from the target. This curious movement causes the striking arm to unroll outwards. During delivery, weight comes down on the front leg and the upper body leans slightly forwards. Because of this combination, back fist can outrange a reverse punch.

FIGS. 21A, B AND C
This is a very good attack sequence with a back fist. The fighter on the left leads with a reverse punch feint which brings the opponent's front arm downwards in a block. Note that the reverse punch does not use a great deal of penetration and there is little chance of the opponent skipping back out of range.

FIG. 21C

Once the opponent's front arm has been brought down with the block, the fighter on the left quickly pulls back the feint reverse punch and strikes to the side of his opponent's head with a back fist.

This sequence is useful when the two contestants are fairly close.

A point worth remembering is that back fist is relatively easy to block and in a simultaneous score situation with a reverse punch, it may not be seen and be discounted.

When the range is slightly greater, a reverse punch can be added to the sequence, immediately following the back fist.

FIGS. 22A, B AND C
In this sequence it is possible to score, but because of the fighter on the right's bad line the chance of success is reduced. Note that his front foot is between his opponent's as he feints with the reverse punch. The follow-up back fist is blocked and an opening is created for a final reverse punch. Unfortunately, because of the bad line used, the opponent also sees a target and is just as correctly placed to use a reverse punch.

When this situation arises the result will be one of three things: either the attacker gets the reverse punch to score, or both punch at the same time and there is no score for either, or the opponent gets his reverse punch in first.

FIGS. 23A, B, C AND D
To increase scoring potential the starting line must be good. The fighter on the right changes his stance to southpaw, so that they

FIG. 22A

FIG. 22B

FIG. 22C

50

FIG. 23A

FIG. 23B

FIG. 23C

FIG. 23D

are almost standing toe-to-toe, and slightly to the outside of the opponent's front foot.

From this start position the attack sequence is launched with a feint reverse punch followed by back fist. In this case, though, the back fist is delivered from a stance more to the side of the opponent who, as a consequence, sees no clear target. The final reverse punch delivery keeps to the outside of the opponent's front foot and ensures that there is no counter to worry about.

FIG. 24A

FIG. 24B

Front Kick

The front kick is one of the first kicking techniques taught to beginners starting karate and yet it is not used a great deal in competition. The reason for this is that at some stage or another students injure their toes using it and thereafter there is a great reluctance to use it. The front kick is a very precise attack which goes direct into the target. By comparison, a roundhouse kick curves in a circular path and is quite likely to catch arms or elbows on the way in.

In order to develop a good front kick the fighter must use a bag. Penetration is necessary and this is difficult to achieve with fighters who only practise against the empty air. It is quite common to see 'empty-air front kicks' skate up the front of an intended target completely missing it!

Another advantage in using the bag is that it gets the toes back out of harm's way. A good tip is to keep the toes relaxed rather than pulling them back. Provided the angle of the kick is correct and the toes relaxed they will flex back automatically on impact. It is a good idea to practise the kick slowly. Not only does this strengthen leg muscles, it also improves balance. Fast snap kicks can disguise a basic imbalance that a slow practise delivery shows up.

FIGS. 24A AND B
During the front kick the kicking foot is quickly brought to its target height by lifting the knee. From this position, the kick is powered all the way out to the target, letting the heel lie slightly lower than the ball of the foot.

FIGS. 25A AND B
To increase the chance of a score with front kick, it should be aimed off centre of the opponent's body. If the kick is targeted to just under

the opponent's front arm, it will be more difficult to block than if it were put in dead-centre.

FIG. 26
Aiming the kick high into the body also makes it more difficult to block.

There is a tendency with younger fighters to use kicks where they are inappropriate. When in punching range, a punch should be used and not a kick. Kicks are useful where there is distance to be covered, since they outrange arm techniques.

FIGS. 27A, B, C, D AND E
The fighter on the right is too far away to deliver an effective front kick. To close the distance he has to lean back and push the hips forward. This makes the kick very unstable and leads to a heavy and uncontrolled landing on the front foot. An alert opponent watches for the foot landing and is able to sweep it, thus breaking balance. The unbalanced attacker is then wide open to a reverse punch score.

FIG. 25A

FIG. 26

FIG. 25B

FIG. 27A

FIG. 27B

FIG. 27C

FIG. 27D

FIG. 27E

FIG. 28A

FIG. 28B

FIG. 28C

FIG. 29A

FIG. 29B

FIGS. 28A, B AND C

When the range is too great for a normal front kick, distance can be covered by means of a drag on the supporting leg as the kicking foot begins to drive in to the target. The lifting of the kicking knee is used as the impetus for the drag and the distance covered is sufficient to bring the kick into effective range without any unbalancing lean or over-extension.

FIGS. 29A, B AND C

Where the distance is even greater, the drag can be changed into a hop forwards, with the kick being delivered upon landing. For the purposes of clarity, the photograph shows quite a high leap, though this is not actually desirable: the purpose of the hop is to close distance and it is therefore a jump forwards and not upwards.

The impetus for the hop forwards again comes from the lifting kicking leg. In all examples of front kick the kicking knee is always raised high and the front hand guard held well out from the body. In this configuration there is little opportunity for the opponent to see and attack a body target.

FIG. 29C

FIG. 30A   FIG. 30B   FIG. 30C

One-step front kicks should be avoided wherever possible. It is always a good idea to get into the correct stance and distance for the kick beforehand. Where a step is inevitable, then it should be disguised by means of an opening feint.

FIGS. 30A, B AND C

Conversely, a short-range front kick needs no body movement at all. The upper body is held perfectly still and the guard remains unchanged, with the front hand well to the front. Keeping the weight back on the supporting leg, the kick is driven out to the target and there are many follow-up options. If the opponent blocks the kick and makes to counter, the kicking leg can be quickly pulled back and the original stance resumed. If conditions are favourable, the kick can fall forwards and a powerful snap punch delivered on landing.

When using the short-range front kick, it is important to remember the two hints on targeting: aim high and aim to the side of the body. A deflection of the correctly targeted front kick will drop it to the outside of the opponent's front foot where it can be used as a footsweep.

FIG. 31

An interesting form of front kick is practised in the Shukokai school of karate. This kick starts in the normal way but during delivery the supporting leg swivels slightly and for the last foot or so of travel the foot curves in to the target. This technique is useful when kicking to the opponent's closed side.

Front kicks can also be delivered off the front foot. This technique is very useful when the attacker rushes in with a snap punch to the face. It is important to keep the guard positioned well in front of the body and close to the kicking knee, so that the body is not opened

FIG. 31

FIG. 32A

FIG. 32B

FIG. 32C

FIG. 32D

FIG. 32E

to counter. As in all previous cases, the kick must fall to the outside of the opponent's front foot.

FIGS. 32A, B, C, D AND E

The power generated by the lifting knee can be used in other than straightforward hops. A sideways or diagonal hop is very useful when line is important. The fighter on the right is a southpaw. The attacker prepares to front kick by raising the knee and then uses this movement to hop diagonally out. This sudden change in line momentarily opens up the opponent for a front kick, or a round-house kick.

In this particular case a straightforward hop would have opened the attacker to a reverse punch strike. The diagonal body movement, however, would tend to make this counter miss.

FIG. 33A

FIG. 33B

FIG. 33C

Roundhouse Kick

The roundhouse kick is one of the most commonly used techniques in competition karate. Unlike in traditional karate, the impact is almost always made with the instep. It is important not to lift up the kicking leg and swing it around in a wide arc to the target: this is very wasteful of energy and telegraphs the technique from the earliest point. The body must not be kept upright or hinged forwards. In both of these instances the range of the kick is foreshortened and the body placed in a more accessible position for a counter.

Regardless of whether a short- or long-range roundhouse kick is used, the body must lean back out of harm's way and the knee must be brought quickly up and across the body. In this position a sudden counterattack by the opponent is brought up short. As with the front kick, the guard must be held well out from the body and there must be little gap between the fending knee and the leading hand.

The lifting knee allows a drag, or hop, to be employed to close range. It is, however, very important to aim at a target. The roundhouse kick suffers more than most techniques in being used when there is no actual target for it.

The kick must also be powered all the way out to the target. In many schools of karate students are taught to power the kick only so far towards the target and after that point, a passive whiplash action takes it in to its target and back again. It is far better to power the kick all the way because this allows not only a greater accuracy but it also makes possible double kicks on the same leg.

FIGS. 33A, B AND C
Here the attacker is in bad line as he attempts to use a roundhouse

FIG. 34A

FIG. 34B

FIG. 34C

kick. Moreover, as he kicks he hinges his body forward and upright so the opponent is presented with a clear target for attack with a reverse punch.

FIGS. 34A, B AND C
In contrast the line used here is correct and the body leans back and away from the possibility of a counterattack. The high knee fends off the opponent and the well-established guard reinforces the defence. Even if the opponent does try to reverse punch, there literally is no target to go for.

FIGS. 35A, B AND C
Great care is needed when attacking a southpaw with a roundhouse kick off the back leg. Even if the line is just right, the attacker can't help momentarily turning square-on. Before the knee can rise to the fend position, a fast reverse puncher can quickly slide in and counter. When using a roundhouse kick against a southpaw, it is better either to use a step-up roundhouse kick or to step out of line, as shown on page 61.

Returning now to the powered double-kick principle, it is always better to kick low first then high. The reason for this is that when kicking low a reserve of foot swivel and hip twist can be maintained and used for the second, higher kick. The second kick uses up the reserve of the movement in order to get the height required. A sequence which starts with a high kick and switches to a lower one is not so easy because the high kick uses up all the hip twist and there is none left for the second.

FIGS. 36A, B, C, D, E AND F
Here a step-up roundhouse kick is used. Guard is maintained and a feint diverts attention momentarily. The first kick smacks hard

FIG. 36A

FIG. 36B

FIG. 36C

FIG. 36D

FIG. 36E

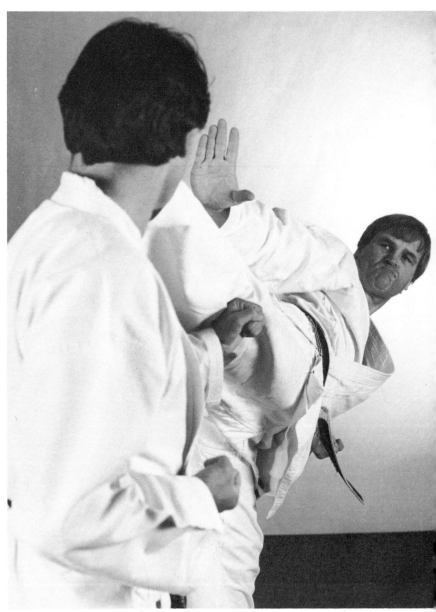

FIG. 36F

against the opponent's calf, giving the impression of being a potential footsweep. Note how the attacker's guard continues to be held well out from the body.

Following the first contact, the kick is quickly withdrawn and the knee rises to a high fend position, with a closed guard. The second kick is then delivered to the side of the head.

Front-foot roundhouse kicks are extensively used and the step-up in conjunction with a feint must be rigorously practised. It is possible to drag the supporting leg slightly if there is a need to slightly increase the range.

FIG. 37A

FIG. 37B

FIG. 37C

Side Kick and Back Kick

Side kicks are occasionally used in competition karate. There are two types. The lesser-used type comes off the back leg and employs a combination swivel on the supporting leg coupled with a thrust out of the heel. The body lies well back from the opponent and the kick can cover a good distance.

FIGS. 37A, B AND C
More frequently used is the side kick that comes off the front leg. The front kicking knee is raised very high and as the foot is driven out there may be a drag on the supporting leg. The drag produces momentum behind the strike, making it very powerful.

The side kick is very useful against an opponent who moves back. Because the kick just keeps on coming, the back step may not be quite far enough. The best time to employ a side kick is when the front leg is past the opponent's forward guard.

FIGS. 38A, B, C AND D
Back kick is less frequently seen. It is quite a difficult kick to perform and needs a great deal of room. Those fighters that can use it effectively are recommended to use it infrequently, otherwise opponents will soon be on the lookout for it. To deliver the kick requires that the hips turn away from the opponent, so the back is momentarily turned. To reduce the chance of a counterattack at this point, the body lies away from the opponent's reach. As with the side kick, it seems to keep on coming and the opponent's backwards jump may not take him quite far enough.

A good time to use a back kick is when the fighter has been pushed to the area perimeter. In this case, it is a worthwhile idea to feint with a reverse punch, then spin around and launch the back kick. In competition karate the head should always turn to look over the shoulder during the kick.

FIG. 38A

FIG. 38B

FIG. 38C

FIG. 38D

Reverse Roundhouse Kick

The reverse roundhouse kick is a spectacular technique which, if successful, will almost certainly score a full point. It is very definitely a move for those fighters who like using feet techniques. The target for the kick is the side of the opponent's face.

FIGS. 39A, B AND C

For competition purposes the kick can be split into two parts: the first is a fast upwards diagonal kick and the second part is a hook that brings the sole of the foot around and back in to the face. A straight leg swing should not be used since this is both slow and difficult to control.

To maximize success with this technique, the starting line is important and the attacker should stand to the outside of his opponent's front foot. During delivery of the kick, the body leans well back from a possible counter and the forward guard is held well out and close to the kicking leg.

FIGS. 40A, B, C AND D

It is never a good idea to use a straightforward reverse roundhouse kick from the back leg when facing an aggressive counterattack. It

FIG. 39A

FIG. 39B

FIG. 39C

FIG. 40A

FIG. 40B

FIG. 40C

FIG. 40D

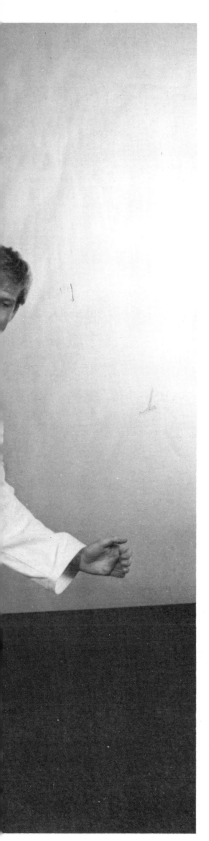

is all too easy for the opponent to move in just as the kick is rising into its target and seize the kicker in a takedown technique.

FIGS. 41A, B, C AND D

A safer way of using reverse roundhouse kick is in the form of a step-up. The fighter on the right stands toe-to-toe, or slightly outside of his opponent's line. From this position, a short reverse punch diverts attention downwards and this is quickly followed by a snap punch. During the snap punch there is no forward body movement and the punch itself is aimed to the side of the opponent's face, causing overblocking. As the snap punch is withdrawing, there is a quick step-up and the reverse roundhouse is delivered from the front foot. Note how the body leans away and the guard is held close.

Even if the opponent were to try a reverse punch, there would be no target for it.

FIG. 41A

FIG. 41B

FIG. 41C

FIG. 41D

FIG. 42A

FIG. 42B

FIG. 42C

FIG. 42D

Changing Kicks

Changing kicks is all about kicks that start off as one technique and finish up as another. It is intended to confuse the opponent and provoke a response which is not appropriate to the final kick used.

FIGS. 42A, B, C AND D
The fighter on the right begins what looks like a normal front kick. The opponent responds by dropping his front arm into a block – except that the kick suddenly changes and becomes a roundhouse kick to the head. The change from one to the other is brought about by the supporting leg suddenly swivelling and the half-extended kicking leg arcing around into the side of the face now exposed by the dropped front hand. For this to be effective, the change from one to the other should come as late as possible to allow the deception to become complete.

As with all previous techniques, it is important that correct use is made of line to reduce the effectiveness of any counterattack.

FIGS. 43A, B AND C
A converse to the last technique is the roundhouse kick that abruptly changes into a front kick. The fighter on the right begins what looks like a perfectly ordinary roundhouse kick to the head, with the body leaning back and the knee moving up to the fend position. The opponent's guard rises to meet the anticipated kick, except that all of a sudden the attacker's ankle drops and his body straightens up. The foot is driven out in a straight line and becomes a front kick to the mid-section.

FIGS. 44A, B, C AND D
From a good line, the fighter on the right does what seems to be a step-up side kick. The opponent goes to knock it down – a perfectly valid defence against a side kick but no use at all against a front

FIG. 43A

FIG. 43B

FIG. 43C

FIG. 44A

FIG. 44B

FIG. 44C

FIG. 44D

kick. As the kicking heel passes the opponent's front guard, the hips suddenly swivel back and the body pulls upright, the side kick changing into a front kick.

FIGS. 45A, B, C AND D

The final example in this series concerns a footsweep that fails to work. The fighter on the right uses a normal footsweep off the back leg, but it is seen and avoided by the opponent lifting the threatened leg. The failed footsweep carries on around, pulling the body with it and presenting the attacker's back to the opponent's reverse punch. As the reverse punch begins, the opponent's body squares on and presents a perfect target for a front kick. To achieve the front kick changeover the hips must be swivelled back and the forward hand held in a strong guard.

FIG. 45A

FIG. 45B

FIG. 45C

FIG. 45D

FIG. 46A

FIG. 46B

FIG. 46C

FIG. 46D

80

Blocking Techniques

Blocks are ways in which an incoming technique is deflected from its target. There are many different types of blocks but one of the most unusual is the rear-hand block. It is unusual because most blocks use the front hand as it is further from the body and closer to the attack.

FIGS. 46A, B, C AND D

In this particular technique, however, the attack has got past the front hand. The fighter on the right snap punches to the opponent's face. The opponent drops his stance slightly and moves his face to the side so that the attack misses. The rear hand slaps the punch to one side and the front guard is used as a mid-section snap punch, followed quickly by a reverse punch.

FIGS. 47A, B, C AND D

The rear-hand block can also be used to deal with a front kick. In this sequence the fighter on the left's front foot is in line with his opponent's rear foot. From this angle a front kick will tend to come at the centre of the body because both are fairly square on to each other. As the kick comes in, the opponent drives off his back leg and moves diagonally forwards, fending off the kick with his rear forearm.

It is important to guard the face during this movement since the attacker is likely to flail out when he feels his balance going.

Maintaining the high face guard, the opponent hip-twists suddenly and hooks the attacker's kicking leg as it is landing. This causes the attacker to fall on to his back and a stamp or side kick is used to finish with a full score.

FIG. 47A

FIG. 47B

FIG. 47C

FIG. 47D

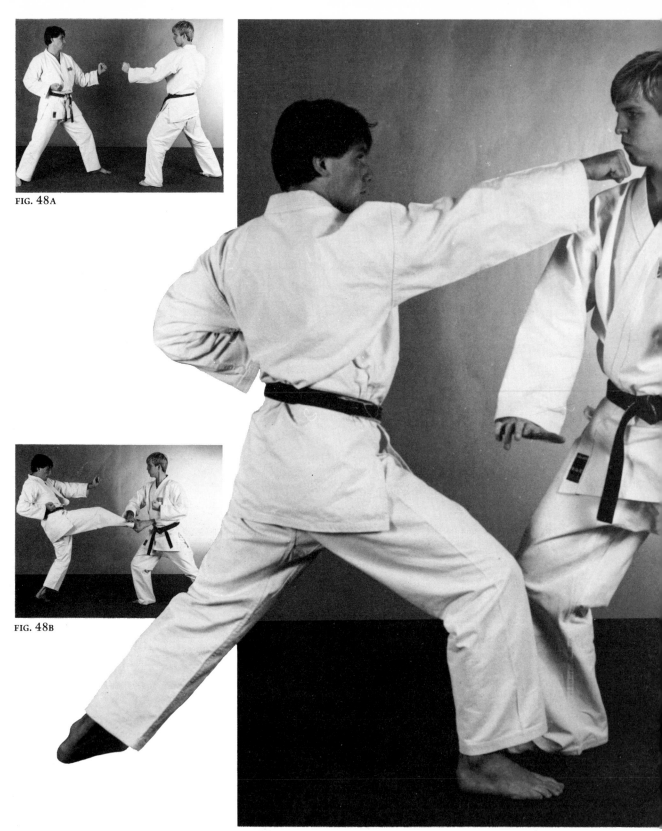

FIG. 48A

FIG. 48B

FIG. 48C

FIGS. 48A, B AND C

The timing of a block can be quite critical and it is better to be early than late. The fighter on the right has blocked his opponent's front kick near the end of its travel. The effect of this is to knock his foot down firmly on to the floor where new-found stability allows him to immediately throw a snap punch.

FIGS. 49A, B, C AND D

Rather than block late, it is a better idea to step back from the kick and let it expire normally. The step back takes the body out of range and a further margin of safety can be employed by pulling the posture into back stance as he lands. In the instant the attacker lands, the opponent transfers weight forwards and uses a reverse punch. This technique is especially good for a smaller person fighting a larger.

FIGS. 50A AND B

Here is an example of an effective early block. This requires a great deal of courage. As the attacker's knee rises into a front-kick delivery, the opponent slides forwards on his front leg and bars the

FIG. 49A

FIG. 49B

FIG. 49C

FIG. 49D

FIG. 50A

FIG. 50B

FIG. 51A

FIG. 51B

FIG. 51C

FIG. 51D

FIG. 51E

FIG. 52A

FIG. 52B

FIG. 52C

kick with a front forearm whilst simultaneously using reverse punch to the attacker's mid-section.

FIGS. 51A, B, C, D AND E

In exactly the same manner as in the previous sequence, a round-house kick that is blocked late can cause problems. In this instance, the fighter on the right throws a high roundhouse kick. The opponent blocks the kick close to its intended target and this allows the foot to fall to the outside of his foot. From here the attacker can easily hook his opponent's front leg and follow with a reverse punch for a full point.

FIGS. 52A, B AND C

More correctly, the roundhouse kick is blocked by a forward guard, well out from the defender's body. This early block causes the kicker to become unbalanced and he is then open to a reverse punch counter.

FIGS. 53A AND B

To block a low roundhouse kick is extremely difficult and it is not advisable to stand still since it can easily curl around the guard and strike to the unguarded back. To avoid this happening, the opponent should jump into the mid-line and block the kick with the front guard. A reverse punch or front kick counter is a useful conclusion to the sequence.

FIGS. 54A, B, C AND D

The technique shown here is particularly good for southpaws facing an orthodox fighter. As the attacker uses front kick off his back leg, the opponent pulls back into cat stance and deflects the kick with the front arm. This arm continues travelling in a circle and becomes a snap punch as the cat stance changes to a forward stance.

FIG. 53A

FIG. 53B

FIG. 54A

FIG. 54B

FIG. 54C

FIG. 54D

FIG. 55A

FIG. 55B

FIG. 55C

FIG. 55D

The deflection of the attacker's foot is important. It must be dropped to the outside of the opponent's. The line is important since it allows the opponent's front foot to slide forward unhindered whilst preventing the attacker from countering effectively.

FIGS. 55A, B, C AND D

This sequence uses a block from orthodox stance. The attacker's front kick is met with a normal hip twist movement and forearm parry. However, in this block the forearm is facing downwards. The effect of this is to prime the arm for a back fist strike to the attacker's face.

It is always a good idea to use the weapon which is closest to the target, and in this case the back fist is set up just right by the block. As a final move, a reverse punch can be used to the attacker's back. A combination of both strikes is more likely to achieve a full point than one alone.

Legsweeps and Hooks

A hook is a foot technique that traps the opponent's lower leg and pulls it in a direction of weakness. A sweep, on the other hand, takes the form of a good solid smack to the lower leg which actually knocks it out of stance. Both hooks and sweeps are delivered with the sole of the foot or the instep.

FIG. 56A

As is the case with many techniques, these should be used only where there is a target. The fighter looks for stances which are too narrow, too wide, or the opponent is just about to land after a kick, or step forward. These cases are suitable for a footsweep or hook whereas a heavy and solidly planted opponent in a good stance is not.

The simplest form of footsweep uses the rear leg. The guard is left well forward and the fighter's body leans away as he sweeps to the opponent's front leg. Power is generated in the small of the back and the sole of the foot hits the target. If the sweep is successful, it is important to have a scoring technique ready since no points are awarded for a sweep on its own.

FIG. 56B

It is also important to work out where the opponent will fall, so as to be correctly positioned to deliver the scoring technique. Many a sweep or hook has been more successful than was anticipated and the opponent landed too far away to be caught before the referee called a halt. To confirm which way the fighter must move, it is a good idea to wait a split-second before going in. This simple precaution will prevent the attacker from running on to a technique if the sweep has been unsuccessful.

There are two other points to be considered. The first is that when an opponent is unbalanced he will very often flail his arms about and the attacker must keep a good face guard. The second point is

Fig. 56c

FIG. 57A

FIG. 57B

92

FIG. 58A

FIG. 58B

FIG. 58C

FIG. 58D

that if the sweep has failed the attacker must move back out to a safe distance and not remain trading punches.

FIGS. 56A, B AND C

The fighter on the right has successfully swept his opponent. The attacker's high guard can clearly be seen protecting his face. Unfortunately, the attacker has not worked out which way the opponent is going to fall and has allowed his footsweep to land well forward, instead of bringing it back. As a result, the opponent has fallen slightly behind the attacker and is impossible to reach with a quick follow-up.

FIGS. 57A, B AND C

The attacker has again successfully swept his opponent, but this time he brings his sweeping foot back. Because of this, the opponent literally falls at his feet and a scoring technique can quickly be used.

FIGS. 58A, B, C, D AND 59A, B, C AND D

In this pair of sequences a hook is used instead of a sweep. The attacker on the right has started from a good line and opens the

FIG. 59A

FIG. 59B

FIG. 59C

FIG. 59D

sequence with a reverse punch. During the punch the attacker slides forward on his front foot until it comes to rest outside the opponent's. From this position the attacker's foot hooks around the back of the opponent's ankle and draws it out.

As with the sweep, the guard is held quite high to protect the face against wild arm swings. The opponent, however, has fallen away from the attacker and when the latter runs in, he is fended off with a kick and the chance of a score is ruined.

If the hook is applied correctly, the opponent's leg must be drawn up high. When this is done, he falls at the attacker's feet and a follow-up is immediately possible.

FIGS. 60A, B, C AND D

The scoring follow-up need not always be a reverse punch. A fighter with supple hips can easily use a stamp, or axe kick. The fighter on the right has attacked with a reverse punch from good line and followed this with a hook which draws the opponent's foot up high.

The attacker's foot continues to rise and then stamps down with an

FIG. 60A

FIG. 60B

FIG. 60D

. 60c

axe kick on the fallen opponent. The use of such a spectacul:
technique increases the chance of receiving a full point score.

FIGS. 61A, B, C, D AND E

In this sequence the opponent is seen to have a poor stance durir
reverse punch. His front knee does not come to lie above his inst
during punching. To use this weakness, the fighter on the l
provides a target. The opponent slides forward and reverse punchd
only to be caught with a hook.

FIG. 61A

FIG. 61B

FIG. 61C

FIG. 61D

FIG. 61E

The hook draws the opponent's foot out in the direction of weakness and drops him to the floor in front of the attacker. Note that the hook used in this sequence is a step-up variant. As with the others, the body leans away and a good guard is maintained by the attacker.

FIGS. 62A, B, C, D AND E
This sequence is a spectacular one, to be used only when well ahead of the opponent. The fighter on the left attacks with a high round-

FIG. 62A

FIG. 62B

G. 62C

FIG. 62D

FIG. 62E

FIG. 63A

FIG. 63B

98

house kick and his opponent simply drops like a stone. From prone position, the opponent strikes the attacker's supporting leg at calf-height.

Because the kick makes the stance unstable, the supporting leg can be easily jarred and the attacker loses balance. Obviously the opponent cannot use a follow-up punch, so he uses the sweeping leg to deliver an axe kick.

FIGS. 63A, B, C AND D

This sequence is very good for attacking an opponent who is in a high stance. The attacker hits the front of the opponent's shin with the sole of his foot. Note the attacker's high guard and body leaning away. The impact against the shin knocks the opponent's foot straight back into his other leg and he consequently sweeps himself!

It is important for the attacker to quickly withdraw his sweeping leg in preparation for the follow-up. The opponent literally falls flat on his face, with head towards the attacker. A reverse punch then completes the sequence.

FIGS. 64A, B, C, D AND E

Sometimes it is possible to footsweep someone in a strong stance. This is done by means of a double-action sweep. In this sequence the attacker strikes to the inside of the opponent's leg with his instep. The impact is not hard enough to unbalance the opponent, but it causes him to resist the impact by leaning into it.

The first sweep is withdrawn right back with a jump and the hips swivel around the reverse way. A second footsweep is then delivered to the other side of the opponent's front leg. If the two sweeps are put in quickly, one after the other, then the resistance made to the first sweep by the opponent helps the second one to be effective.

FIG. 63C

FIG. 63D

FIG. 64A

FIG. 64B

FIG. 64C

FIG. 64D

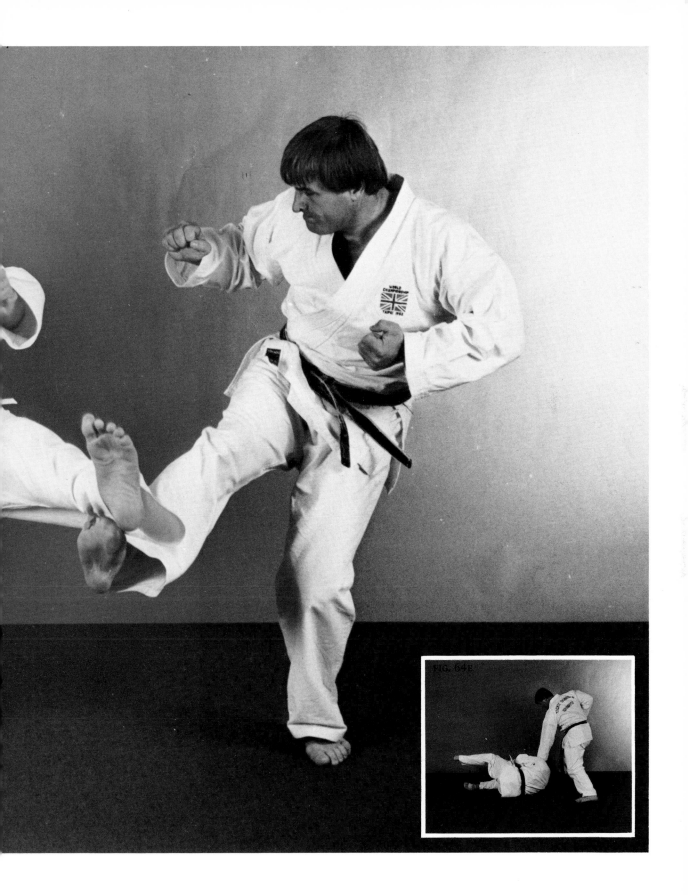

FIG. 64E

As with all sweeps, the attacking leg is returned to its original position and a follow-up reverse punch easily applied.

FIGS. 65A, B, C AND D
Here the first sweep is done from the back leg – instead of in a step-up form. As the sweep hits home, with the sole of the attacker's foot striking the opponent's calf, the latter leans into it. The attacker then quickly withdraws the first sweep and jumps back with the foot, at the same time swivelling his hips the reverse way.

The second footsweep is delivered with the instep against the inside of the opponent's already weakened leg. The leg is knocked outwards and the stance destroyed. It is important to be ready with a fast reverse punch as the opponent is unbalanced.

FIGS. 66A, B, C, D AND E
Footsweeps and hooks can be used as part of combination techniques. The fighter on the left is dealing with an aggressive opponent who attacks with a face punch.

FIG. 66A

FIG. 65A

FIG. 65B

FIG. 65C

FIG. 65D

FIG. 66E

FIG. 66C

FIG. 66D

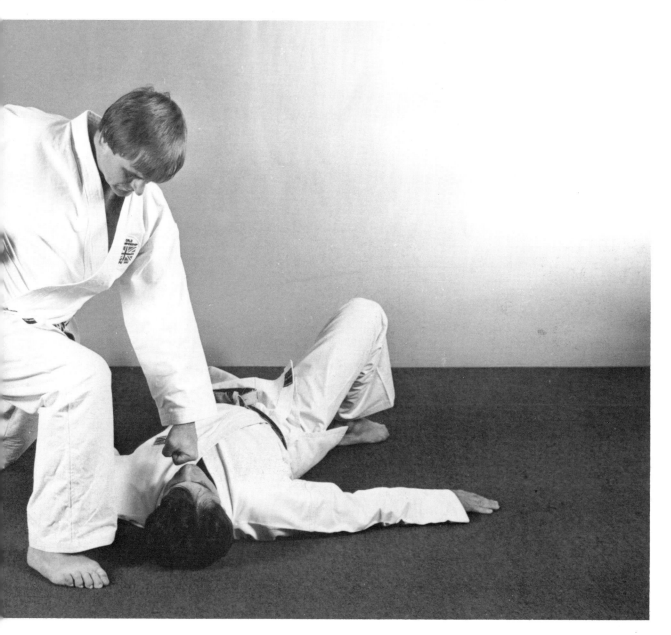

FIG. 67A

FIG. 67B

FIG. 67C

FIG. 67D

FIG. 67E

Leaning back, the fighter front kicks off the front leg. This is a good counter to a snap punch, outranging it and removing the necessity to block. As always, the starting line must be correct and the kick put in to the side of the opponent's body. As the kick drops to the outside of the opponent's front foot, a reverse punch is used followed by a hook.

As previously mentioned, the hook must be lifted high and the stance must be effectively closed against counterattacks. The hooking leg drops back and a reverse punch completes the sequence.

As a final example of a footsweep or hook used as part of a combination, look at sequence 67.

FIGS. 67A, B, C, D, E AND F
Starting from a position of good line, the attacker throws a normal roundhouse kick to the head. Note the body leans away and the effective guard. Following the kick, the attacker is seemingly open to a reverse punch counter. As the punch begins, the attacker knocks it down and simultaneously hooks the front leg up and away with his instep.

The knockdown and hook are simultaneous, causing the opponent to fall onto his back. A reverse punch completes the sequence.

FIG. 68A

FIG. 68B

FIG. 68C

106

Takedown Techniques

Takedown techniques are spectacular moves which literally catch the opponent in mid-technique and up-end him.

3. 68D

FIGS. 68A, B, C, D AND E

The fighter on the right attacks with a front kick. The starting line is such that the kick will come in to the centre of the opponent's body. With a slight sideways movement, the kick is evaded and caught in the crook of the rear elbow. The front arm is extended and used to push the attacker off balance by means of a palm-heel strike.

The opponent takes a step forward behind the shove and the attacker falls over on to his back. A final step forward takes the opponent into reverse punch range.

3. 68E

When practising this technique the opponent must remember to keep advancing, otherwise the situation degenerates into a wrestling match with no scores possible.

FIGS. 69A, B, C, D AND E

This second example of a takedown technique uses the opponent's own strength and speed against him. The fighter on the right starts from a southpaw stance with good line. The attack takes the form of a front kick and it is countered by body evasion. The rear foot crosses behind the front foot and the kicking leg is caught with the rear hand in an over-the-top grasp. The front hand reaches through and under the opponent's rear armpit.

Using the step across and hip movement to power the technique, the opponent is twisted around and unbalanced by jarring his thigh with the attacker's leg. This drops him on to his back and open to

FIG. 69A

FIG. 69B

FIG. 69C

69D

69E

a reverse punch. The opponent's leg is firmly held, so as to prevent him from rolling away and out of reach.

Once a degree of skill has been reached in this technique, it becomes possible to take a really fast kick and dump the attacker on his backside with no effort at all.

The next example of a takedown involves an apparent paradox. On page 33 readers were advised never to let their kicks fall inside the opponent's front foot. This is usually the case, except for this one deliberate technique.

FIGS. 70A, B, C, D AND E

The attack is delivered from a southpaw stance and the fighter on the right performs a step-up front kick. The kick is aimed more to the opponent's body rather than under his front arm and, as a result, it falls to the inside of his front leg.

As the weight comes down, however, the attacker's front arm grasps the opponent's shoulder. In a simultaneous movement the

FIG. 70A

FIG. 70B

70C

FIG. 70D

FIG. 70E

FIG. 71A

FIG. 71B

FIG. 71C

kicking leg is driven back into the opponent's front leg and he is pulled down by the grasp on his shoulder.

The effect of this is to tumble the opponent over the attacker's front leg and a follow-up reverse punch can be used.

It must be emphasized that the whole sequence is deliberate and it is not just a case of making the best of a bad situation. The front kick is not intended to score but merely to divert attention and prepare the positioning.

FIGS. 71A, B, C, D AND E
This is the converse to sequence 70. In this case the attacker is in a normal stance and has good line. He front kicks from his back leg and deliberately aims to the side of his opponent's body.

The attacker then lets the weight of the spent kick bring his leg down, but before his foot touches the mat he suddenly hooks it back and strikes the opponent in the chest with a palm heel. The attacker has literally thrown himself off balance with this move and can only regain stability through the impact on the opponent's chest.

As the opponent tumbles, the hooking leg is taken straight back so that the distance and position are correct for a reverse punch.

FIGS. 72A, B, C, D, E AND F
The next takedown sequence is quite spectacular and relies upon a circular movement. The fighters face each other in normal stances and the one on the right attacks with a footsweep from his back leg. The opponent sees the sweep and lifts his leg clear of danger, but the attacker keeps on turning in the direction of the apparently failed sweep.

FIG. 71D

FIG. 71E

FIG. 72A

FIG. 72B

FIG. 72C

FIG. 72D

The sweeping leg drops well forward and the attacker's hips continue rotating. This combined forward body movement and spin cause the attacker to bump into the opponent, jarring him. At the same instant, the trailing leg sweeps the opponent's already weakened supporting leg and he falls up and back.

The attacker draws up the sweeping leg and completes the sequence with a stamp kick.

During the spin into the opponent the attacker keeps a good guard and is always looking at his opponent, so that distance can be correctly judged.

FIGS. 73A, B, C, D, E AND F
The last in the series of takedowns uses a counter to a roundhouse kick. As the kick comes in, the opponent steps into it, bending both knees, and fends it off with an extended front arm. The bent knees are then used to drive the opponent into the attacker and the blocking arm is withdrawn and extended under the attacker's leading armpit.

FIG. 72E

FIG. 72F

113

FIG. 73A

FIG. 73B

FIG. 73C

The opponent's front leg lifts forward and out and then swings back into the attacker's supporting leg, knocking it backwards. The opponent, maintaining his hold on the attacker, leans forward and dumps the latter on his back. A reverse punch completes the sequence.

FIG. 73D

FIG. 73E

FIG. 73F

Combination Techniques

FIG. 74A

These are legion and only a few can be shown in this book. The idea of a combination technique is to provoke a response, or a target, by means of a series of techniques. In the first example (74) a back fist is used to set up the opponent for a roundhouse kick.

FIGS. 74A, B, C AND D
A straightforward roundhouse kick can have its chance of success improved if it is used in a combination such as this. The fighter on the right is in a southpaw stance and leans forward to deliver a back fist from the front hand. This comes in to the side of the opponent's face and causes him to over-block.

The over-blocking obscures the opponent's view of the step-up that immediately follows the back fist and the subsequent roundhouse kick finds an open target.

The back fist is only a feint, delivered to the opponent's guard. There is no attempt to range it accurately, since this may well bring the attacker into the opponent's reverse punch range.

FIGS. 75A, B, C, D AND E
This next combination technique sequence is slightly more elaborate and shows how it is possible to add on techniques.

Both fighters are in the same stance and the one on the right leans in with a snap punch to the opponent's face. No attempt is made to close the range since this is merely a feint, setting up the opponent for the final score. After the snap punch, a reverse punch is launched and again there is no attempt made to close the range.

The opponent may well block both techniques and will find the high/low targeting disconcerting. The reverse punch takes advan-

FIG. 74D

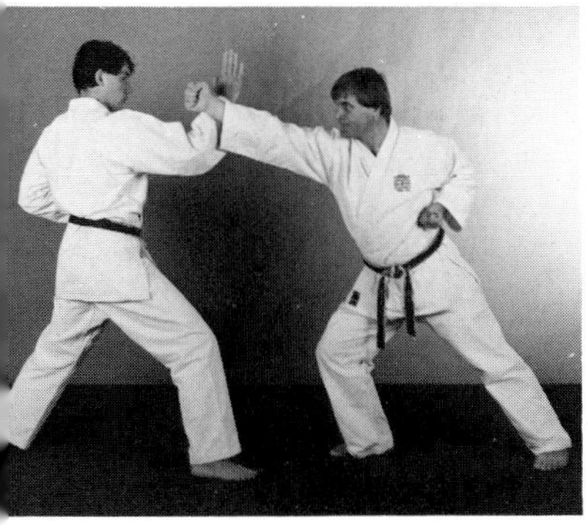

;. 74B

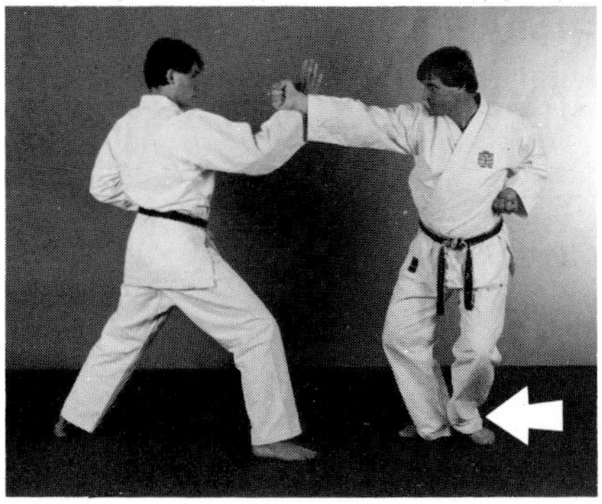

FIG. 74C

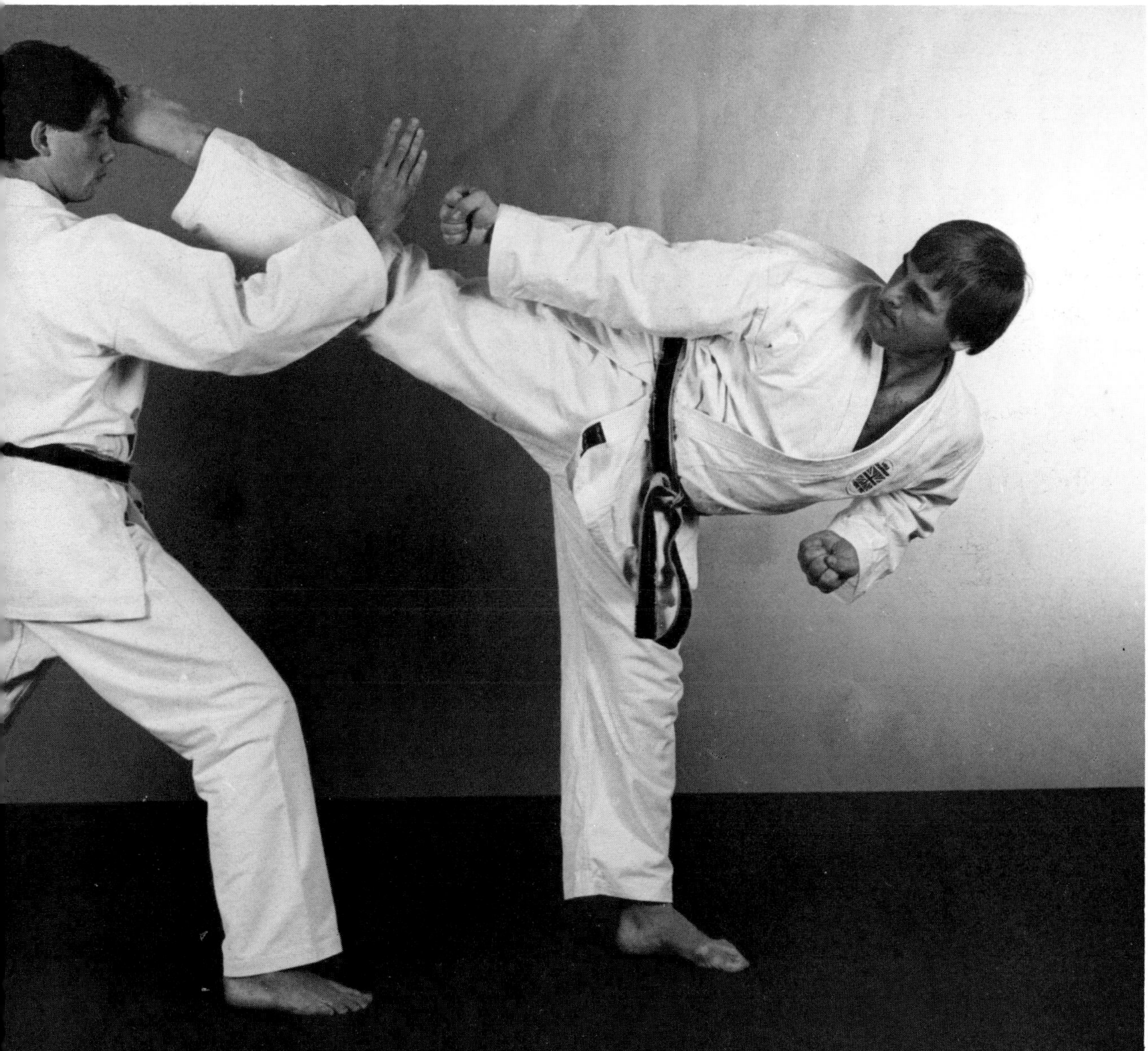

FIG. 75A

FIG. 75B

FIG. 75C

FIG. 75D

tage of the momentary confusion to step up and deliver a high roundhouse kick to the now-undefended head.

It is important to note that the guard is maintained during the step-up and the body leans well out of harm's way during the kick.

FIGS. 76A, B, C, D, E, F, G AND H
Building further on the combinations used, the fighter on the right quickly steps up and delivers a high roundhouse kick. The kick is,

3. 75E

119

however, intentionally out-of-range and smacks into the opponent's front hand. Without closing the distance significantly, it drops down forward and is immediately followed by a snap punch and a reverse punch.

As before, these two punches are deliberately short and do not frighten the opponent into stepping back. A very fast final roundhouse kick is very much in range and strikes to the opponent's mid-section or head. This last roundhouse technique must be delivered from a good line.

FIG. 76A

FIG. 76B

FIG. 76C

FIG. 76D

FIG. 76E

FIG. 76F

FIG. 76G

FIG. 76H

FIG. 77A

FIG. 77B

FIG. 77C

FIG. 77D

FIG. 77E

FIG. 77F

FIGS. 77A, B, C, D, E, F AND G

In the last of the combination technique sequences the opponent is an aggressive counterpuncher. The fighter on the left opens the sequence with a snap punch. As expected, the opponent blocks this and immediately counters with a reverse punch.

The reverse punch is blocked with the same arm that delivered the snap punch simply by pulling it back and turning the hips. Though it is tempting to follow up with a reverse punch, the blocking arm is closest to a target and so it snaps back out again as the opponent withdraws his failed reverse punch.

FIG. 77G

If the snap punch fails to score, then a reverse punch can be used to follow it. If the opponent has begun to move back, or the reverse punch also fails, then the attacker simply steps up and uses a roundhouse kick to the head.

Whenever a reverse punch fails, it is always a good plan to follow automatically with a step-up roundhouse kick if there is adequate range.